MW00636259

Stargirl

Jerry Spinelli

TEACHER GUIDE

NOTE:

The trade book edition of the novel used to prepare this guide is found in the Novel Units catalog and on the Novel Units website. Using other editions may have varied page references.

Please note: We have assigned Interest Levels based on our knowledge of the themes and ideas of the books included in the Novel Units sets, however, please assess the appropriateness of this novel or trade book for the age level and maturity of your students prior to reading with them. You know your students best!

BN 978-1-58130-818-1

To order, contact your
local school supply store, or:

Toll-Free Fax: 877.716.7272
Phone: 888.650.4224
3901 Union Blvd., Suite 155
St. Louis, MO 63115

sales@novelunits.com

novelunits.com

Table of Contents

Skills and Strategies

Thinking
Research, compare/contrast, pros/cons, analysis, creative thinking, critical thinking, brainstorming, predicting

Comprehension
Cause/effect, summarization

Writing
Poetry, essays, journal entries, speeches, letters

Listening/Speaking
Discussion, oral presentation, public speaking

Vocabulary
Word maps, definitions, parts of speech

Literary Elements
Setting, conflict, simile, metaphor, theme, characterization, foreshadowing, point of view

Across the Curriculum
Art—collage, caricatures, sculptures, painting; Drama—reenactments; Music—dance, song lyrics; Math—manipulatives, songs; History—research; Science—research, archaeology

Genre: young adult fiction

Setting: Mica and Phoenix, Arizona; Mica Area High School

Point of View: first-person narrative

Themes: nonconformity, fear of rejection, first love, self-discovery

Conflict: person vs. person, person vs. self; both main characters search for acceptance from others and selves

Tone: informal, upbeat, candid

Summary

In a typical high school where popularity is measured by one's ability to conform, Stargirl stands out like a water lily on the desert sand. Until she manages to achieve cheerleader status, her only friends are Cinnamon (a pet rat that she carries in her sunflower bag) and Dori Dilson. Leo, the story's narrator, is fascinated by Stargirl and eventually begins to date her. Though Stargirl becomes popular for a brief while, her popularity is short-lived, especially because of her propensity to cheer for both teams when at football or basketball games. Her continual challenges of the status quo at Mica Area High School wind her (and Leo) through cycles of acceptance and rejection, while the students at Mica High are discovering more about who they really are and who they want to be.

About the Author

Jerry Spinelli was born in Norristown, Pennsylvania. He attended Gettysburg College and Johns Hopkins University. He and his wife, Eileen (who is also an author), have six children and eleven grandchildren. Jerry Spinelli began writing when he was 16 years old. When a poem he wrote after a baseball game was published in the local newspaper, his dreams turned from professional ballplaying to writing. After writing four adult novels that were never published, he began writing for children. Among Spinelli's books are *Who Put That Hair in My Toothbrush?*, *Maniac Magee* (the 1991 Newbery Medal winner), *Crash*, and *Wringer* (a Newbery Honor book in 1998). Spinelli says that he gets his ideas for books from students and other real-life situations. His autobiography, *Knots in My Yo-Yo String*, was published in 1998.

Major Characters

Leo Borlock: narrator; high school junior; fascinated by Stargirl and eventually becomes her boyfriend; producer/director of *Hot Seat*

Stargirl (Susan) Caraway: the new girl in school; high school sophomore; eccentric; enjoys celebrating others; excellent orator; carries around a pet rat named Cinnamon

Minor Characters

Kevin Quinlan: Leo's best friend; host of *Hot Seat*

A. H. (Archibald Hapwood) Brubaker, aka Archie: retired professor who opens his home to students; loves to teach children who visit his home

Hillari Kimble: popular girl at school who resents Stargirl and believes she is a "fake"

Dori Dilson: besides Leo, Stargirl's only friend for most of the book; is the first person to sit with Stargirl during lunch

Wayne Parr: attractive and popular male at school; outstanding in little but his appearance; Hillari Kimble's boyfriend; ambition in life is to become a model for *GQ* magazine

Mallory Stillwell: pretty, blonde cheerleader captain; invites Stargirl to join the squad

Mr. McShane: one of Stargirl's teachers; sponsors her trip to the state oratorical competition

Initiating Activities

1. Brainstorming: Place the phrase "Fear of Rejection" in the center of the Attribute Web (see page 5 of this guide). Allow students to brainstorm a list of meanings of this phrase.

2. Discussion: Lead a class discussion about the role peer pressure plays at your school. Discuss positive ways of handling peer pressure.

3. Prediction: Select one paragraph at random from the beginning, middle, and end of the book. Read these paragraphs to the students. Based on these three paragraphs, have students predict the plot of the book.

4. Prereading: Ask students if they have read other books by the author, Jerry Spinelli. If so, have the students describe traits about the main characters in his books. Based on this information, have the class predict what traits they believe the main character of *Stargirl* will possess.

5. Prediction: Give students the following list of words: archaeology, peer pressure, young love, shunning, and non-conformity. Ask them to write a short paragraph explaining what they think will happen in the book.

Vocabulary Activities

1. Part of Speech Race: Review the glossary on pages 26–28 of this guide. Randomly select 20 words. Give each student a list of the words and start a timer. The first student to correctly identify the part of speech for each word is the winner.

2. Definition Game: Assign each student a vocabulary word. On a notecard, the student will write three possible definitions of the word. One definition must correctly define the word as it is used in the book. The other two definitions must be incorrect, though sound plausible. Make sure students mark the correct definitions on the cards. Collect the notecards and shuffle them. Then divide the class into two teams. Take turns reading cards to each team. The team has one minute to guess the correct definition and receive two points for every correct answer. The opposing team may earn one point by correctly identifying the definition if the first team's answer is incorrect. Alternate reading cards for each team until all cards have been drawn. The team with the most points wins.

3. Vocabulary Word Map: Assign each student a vocabulary word for which s/he must draw a picture of the definition. Hang the pictures, with the corresponding vocabulary word hanging beneath, on a bulletin board.

4. Vocabulary Story: Place students in groups of five. Assign ten vocabulary words to each group. Give each group 15 minutes to write a short story that includes every vocabulary word. Allow the class to vote on the most creative story. Winning stories must have used each vocabulary word correctly.

5. Unfamiliar Word List: Have students flip through the book and select three words that they have never seen before or for which they do not know the definition. Students should look up these words and define them (as they are used in the book). Then they should write a unique sentence for each word that demonstrates its definition. Collect the words from the students. Make a master list of the unfamiliar words and their definitions. Hand out copies of this list to the students.

Attribute Web

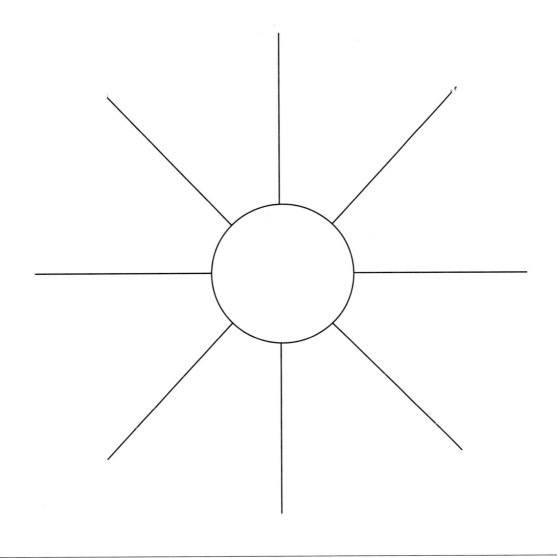

Story Map

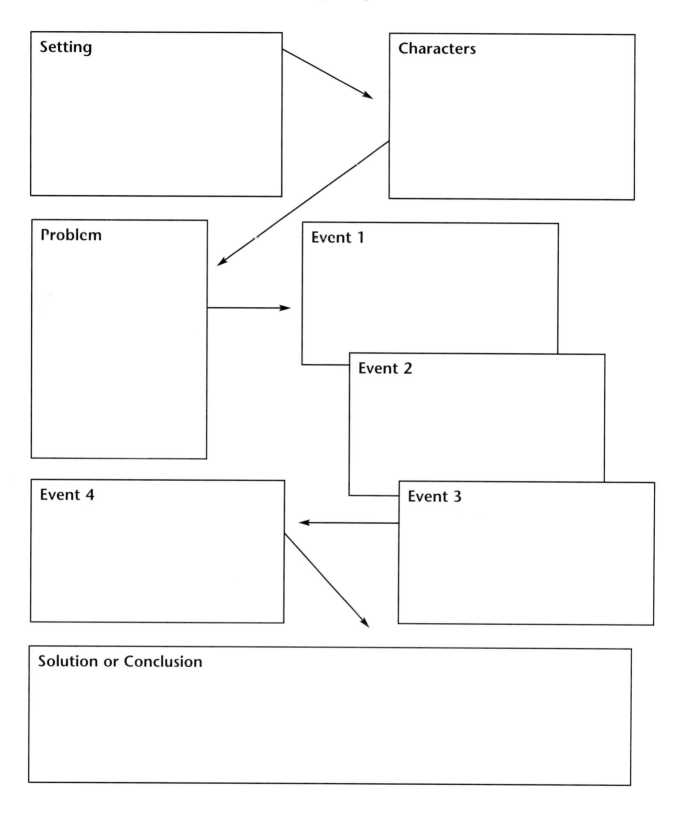

Characterization

Directions: In each oval, write an adjective that describes the character's personality. Then fill in each rectangle with a detail about the character that illustrates that part of the character's personality.

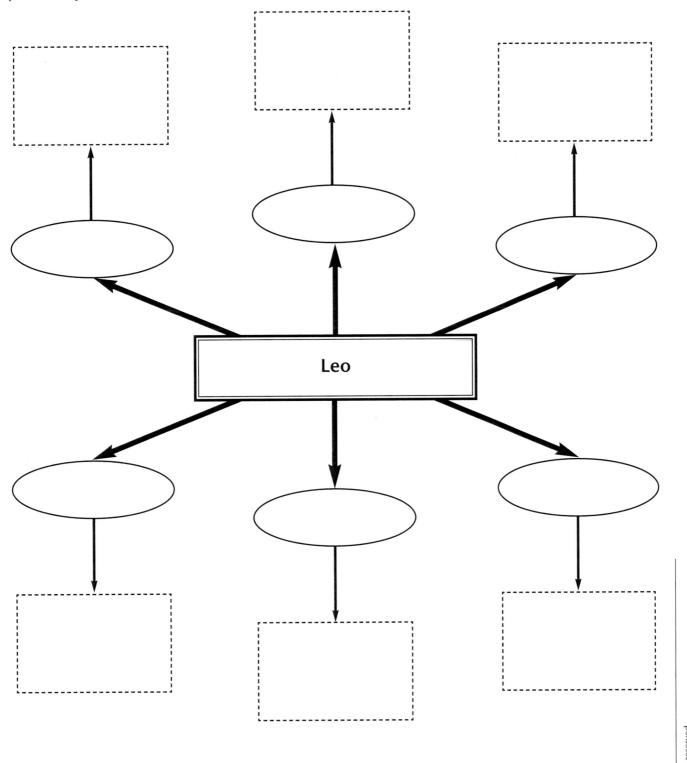

© Novel Units, Inc. | 7

Character Analysis

Directions: Working in small groups, discuss the attributes of the characters listed below. In each character's box, write several words or phrases that describe him or her.

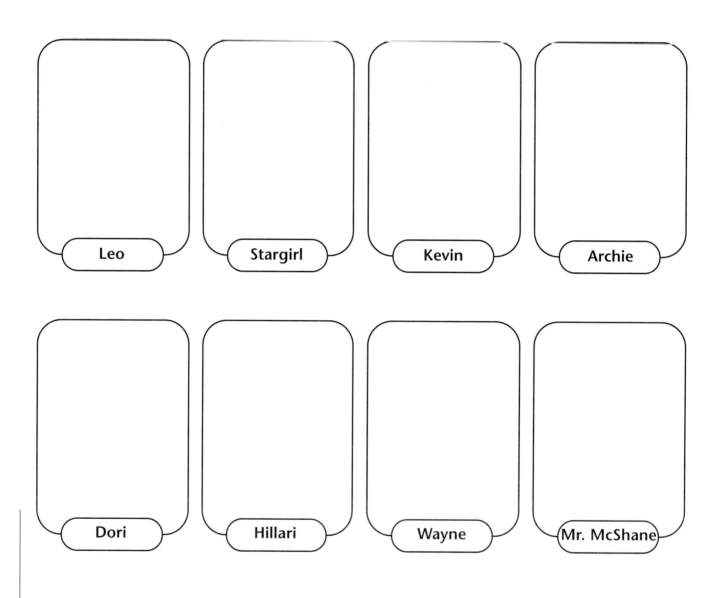

Leo

Stargirl

Kevin

Archie

Dori

Hillari

Wayne

Mr. McShane

Foreshadowing Chart

Foreshadowing is the literary technique of giving clues to coming events in a story.

Directions: Think about *Stargirl*. What examples of foreshadowing do you recall from the story? If necessary, skim through the chapters to find examples of foreshadowing. List at least four examples below. Explain what clues are given, then list the coming event that is suggested.

Foreshadowing	Page #	Clues	Coming Event

Cause and Effect Map

Directions: List one major effect that occurs in *Stargirl* in the Effect box. Then list six events that caused this effect in the rest of the boxes.

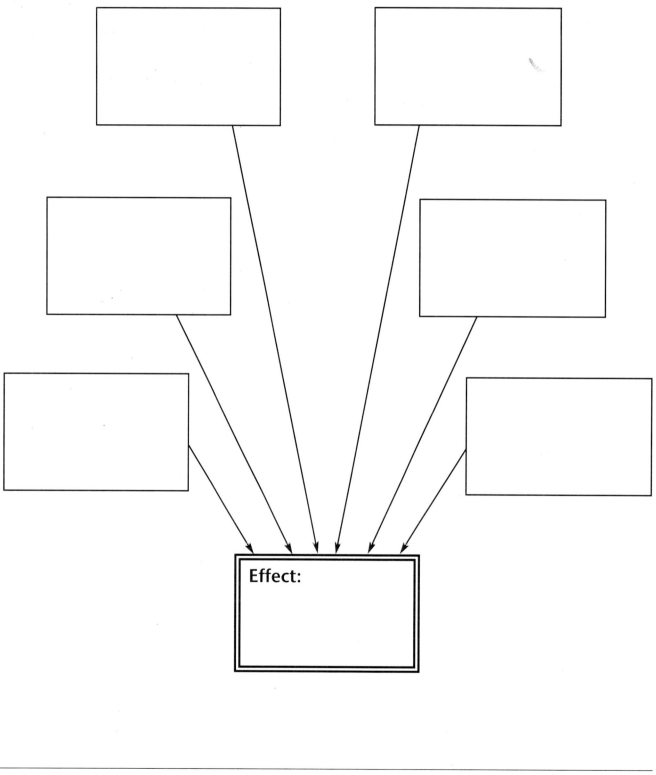

Effect:

Porcupine Necktie–Chapter 2, pp. 1–12

The narrator, high school junior Leo Borlock, is introduced. The school year begins, as does a buzz about the newest student—Stargirl. Stargirl's lack of conformity and her kindness to others make her an enigma to the rest of the student body, who begin to debate about whether or not she is "real." Hillari Kimble emerges as Stargirl's most grievous enemy at Mica High.

Vocabulary
flourish (1)
quills (2)
milling (3)
keener (3)
marooned (4)
plaited (8)
serenaded (10)

Discussion Questions

1. What happens in the opening chapter that attracts the reader's attention? *(Answers may vary, but should include the discussion about a porcupine necktie, the mystery gift, or the statement that someone is watching the narrator. pp. 1–2)*

2. When Stargirl arrives at Mica Area High School, there is a "buzz" in the hallways. Describe what happens at your school when a new person arrives. *(Answers will vary.)*

3. Why do the students believe Stargirl is a "fake"? Do you think she is a fake? Why or why not? *(Answers will vary, but could include her strange clothes, strange hairstyles, that she carries around a pet rat and a ukulele, dances in the rain, sings "Happy Birthday" to complete strangers at lunch, twirls around the lunchroom, says "Hi" even to seniors in the halls, asks questions about trolls in history class, makes up songs in math, etc. Answers will vary.)*

4. Do you agree or disagree with Kevin that Stargirl will not survive at the high school without changing in some way? Why or why not? *(Answers will vary. p. 10)*

5. Why do you think Leo comes to the conclusion that Stargirl is "real" (p. 12)? *(Answers will vary.)*

Supplementary Activities

1. Characterization: Have students begin filling out their Character Analysis charts (see page 8 of this guide). They should continue to add to the charts as they read the book.

2. Literary Devices: Have students keep a list of similes and metaphors as they read. They should add to their list as they read the book. **Similes**—"looked like Heidi. Or Bo Peep" (p. 8); "face...red as...ribbons" (p. 9); "we quickly snapped back into place, like rubber bands" (p. 10); "the fabulous purred on my snow-white sheet like some dark cat come in from the desert" (p. 12) **Metaphor**—"hair was the color of sand" (p. 4)

3. Math/Music: Stargirl writes a song about isosceles triangles (p. 11). Have students write their own songs about two other shapes (square, circle, oval, rectangle, diamond, etc.).

Chapters 3–5, pp. 13–26

Rumors continue to fly about Stargirl, though Leo becomes fascinated by her and follows her one day after school. Kevin and Leo argue about whether or not to ask Stargirl to appear on *Hot Seat*. In the meantime, Wayne Parr appears on the show. Stargirl makes a very expressive appearance during halftime at the school's football game. The next week, many people attend the game to see her, but she does not appear. Finally, Mallory Stillwell, the captain of the cheerleaders, asks Stargirl to join the squad. Stargirl accepts.

Vocabulary
saguaros (14)
balking (14)
amok (14)
perpetual (15)
flitting (15)
aviary (16)
ambition (20)
disdainful (21)
converging (23)
antic (26)

Discussion Questions

1. Why do you think Leo refuses to recruit Stargirl for the Hot Seat? Do you agree or disagree with Leo's point of view? Why or why not? *(Answers will vary. p. 13)*

2. Review the students' theories about Stargirl on page 14 of the novel. How many do you believe are true about her? Discuss why the students create these theories about Stargirl and then list any of your own theories. *(Answers will vary.)*

3. Why does Leo follow Stargirl one day after school? What does he learn about her during that time? *(Answers will vary. pp. 16–18)*

4. How does Leo describe Wayne Parr? Does Wayne remind you of anyone you know? *(not outstanding in anything but appearance, the grand marshal of the daily parade; Answers will vary. pp. 19–21)*

5. Why do so many people flock to the football game after Stargirl's first appearance on the field? *(Answers will vary, but could include a reference to people's fascination with what is different or out of the ordinary. To the citizens of Mica, her potential appearance would have been a form of unusual entertainment. p. 24)*

6. Why do the students seem to be enjoying Stargirl's presence toward the end of Chapter 5? Why are they still keeping their distance? *(Answers will vary, but could include comments about people's desires to be celebrated and the fear of the unknown. pp. 25–26)*

7. **Prediction:** In what way(s) might Stargirl challenge Wayne Parr?

8. **Prediction:** Will Stargirl leave Hillari alone on her birthday?

Supplementary Activities

1. Career/Future: In the book, Leo wants to be a sports announcer, Kevin a talk show host, and Wayne Parr a male model. Ask students to brainstorm a list of careers that interest them. Ask them to list some ways they could prepare for a future career while they are still in elementary or middle school.

2. Writing: Have students compose a journal entry Stargirl may have written the night after she leaves the football stadium.

3. Literary Devices: Have students add to their list of similes and metaphors. Have the students evaluate the literary devices to determine why the author chooses specific analogies to describe people or events. **Similes**—"cactus looked like Ping Pong paddles with whiskers" (pp. 13–14); "pin her to a corkboard like a butterfly" (p. 15); "observed her as if she were a bird in an aviary" (p. 16); "swirled like a dust devil" (p. 22); "marched stiffly like a wooden soldier" (p. 22) **Metaphors**—"She was the faintest scent of a cactus flower, the flitting shadow of an elf owl" (p. 15); "he was grand marshal of our daily parade" (p. 19)

Chapters 6–9, pp. 27–42

Hillari continues to disapprove of Stargirl, especially when Stargirl insists on singing "Happy Birthday" using Hillari's name. Leo and Kevin visit Archie to discuss Stargirl. They find out that Stargirl knows Archie and has been tutored by him for several years and that Stargirl's family life is not that unusual. Before long, Stargirl is the most popular person in school. Leo is not sure to what he should attribute this change in the student body's perception of her and their new appreciation for individual expression.

Vocabulary

ferociously (28)
blithely (28)
creodont (30)
proximity (30)
bafflement (32)
confirmation (32)
charade (39)
acclamation (39)
dormant (40)
amorphous (41)

Discussion Questions

1. Why is Hillari insistent that Stargirl not sing to her on her birthday? *(Answers will vary. p. 27)*

2. Why does Stargirl still decide to sing "Happy Birthday" using Hillari's name while looking at Leo? *(Answers will vary. p. 29)*

3. Describe Archie and his role in Leo, Kevin, and Stargirl's lives. *(Answers will vary, but should include his interest in paleontology, his desire to teach, and the fact that he has tutored Stargirl for the last five years. pp. 31–33)*

4. Evaluate the advice Archie gives to Leo and Kevin regarding *Hot Seat* and Stargirl. Is he a good person for the boys to visit? *(Answers will vary, but could include references to Archie's ability to answer the boys' questions and to challenge them. For example, he tells them a bit about Stargirl's background, but concludes by telling them that they will learn more from their questions than from her answers. He also refuses to tell them whether or not they should invite her to appear on* Hot Seat. *He refers to them as "men" when he tells them to settle their disagreement on their own. pp. 33–35)*

5. Who does Archie think the boys might see if they look at Stargirl long enough? *(Answers will vary. p. 35)*

6. Leo offers four possible reasons why Stargirl becomes popular by December. His four suggestions include Stargirl's cheerleading, Hillari Kimble's backlash, Dori Dilson, and the student population. Evaluate each of Leo's potential reasons. Do you agree with any of them? Do you have an idea of your own for why Stargirl suddenly becomes popular? *(Answers will vary. The most probable reason for Stargirl's popularity is a change in the students. As they change their perception of her, she becomes "popular." pp. 36–39)*

7. Analyze the irony of the statement, "We honored her by imitation" (p. 38). Solicit discussion about whether or not the class thinks Stargirl is flattered or offended when people imitate her. *(Discussion will vary, but should include reference to the fact that Stargirl was unpopular at first because she was different. When the students imitate her, she is no longer unique. pp. 38–39)*

8. Compare and contrast Wayne Parr's influence on the student body at the beginning of the year with Stargirl's influence on the student body toward the end of December. What do Wayne Parr and Stargirl each symbolize? *(Answers will vary, but should include references to the student body mimicking one or the other. However, Wayne Parr represents conformity. He is the symbol of a culture obsessed with appearances and self-absorption. Stargirl represents nonconformity and selflessness. She sparks a "rebellion" by countering their ideas of what is "normal" in the ways that she dresses, acts, gives, and celebrates others.)*

9. **Prediction:** How will Leo be caught in the middle during Stargirl's fall from fame?

Supplementary Activities

1. Drama: Instruct the class to reenact a scene from the high school cafeteria after Stargirl becomes "popular." Encourage students to behave in ways that are appropriate, but different from their normal behavior.

2. Critical/Creative Thinking: Archie seems to be an ideal teacher to many students at Mica Area High School. Instruct students to write an ad for the newspaper that describes their ideal teachers. Each student's description of his or her ideal teacher should explain why the student feels he or she would learn more from this teacher than any other.

3. Literary Devices: Have students add to their list of similes and metaphors. Have students continue to evaluate the literary devices, determining why the author chooses specific analogies to describe people or events. **Simile**—"leading her girlfriends like an invading general" (p. 27) **Metaphor**—"For the dormant mud frogs we had been" (p. 40)

Chapters 10–12, pp. 43–61

Leo and Kevin decide to ask Stargirl to be a guest on *Hot Seat*. Stargirl continues to demonstrate empathy and selflessness. However, her popularity begins to fade as the Electrons grow less tolerant of her choice to cheer for both teams during basketball games. Stargirl's appearance on *Hot Seat* begins with an outstanding pantomime, but Leo is wary of the questions the grim-faced jury may ask her later in the show.

Vocabulary
yielded (43)
lure (43)
banishing (46)
foreground (46)
squabble (47)
mortified (48)
oblivious (50)
hapless (51)
veterans (52)
mock (55)
cued (56)
maestro (58)
pantomime (61)

Discussion Questions

1. Why do you think Stargirl agrees to appear on *Hot Seat*? *(Answers will vary.)*

2. Why does the narrator discuss Stargirl's role at Anna Grisdale's grandfather's funeral and in Danny Pike's homecoming? What might these events foretell with regard to Stargirl's popularity? *(Answers will vary. The narrator continues to point out Stargirl's unusual behavior. The audience is aware that her personality has not altogether changed since becoming popular—she still makes time for others, feels others' pain, and expresses herself in unique ways. pp. 44–47)*

3. On page 51 of the novel, Leo explains the transformation of the student body's school spirit once the basketball team begins to win. Why does the school's obsession with winning seem to influence the way the students treat Stargirl? Do you agree or disagree with their behavior? *(Answers will vary. Note that Stargirl's behavior, which contradicts the student body's complete disdain for the opposition, challenges the way the students expect each other to act. Her nonconformity is no longer appreciated because the students want to unite only in support of their sports team.)*

4. Do you agree with Leo that bad things don't seem to "stick" to Stargirl? *(Answers will vary. pp. 52–53)*

5. Discuss the difference between the roles of "Chico," Leo, and Kevin on *Hot Seat*. Which role is most appealing to you? *("Chico" runs the camera, Leo is the director who orders certain camera shots and oversees what images are depicted on the screen, and Kevin is the host who is in the spotlight and must mediate between the guests and jury. Answers will vary. pp. 55–58)*

6. Prediction: After Stargirl's seemingly great beginning on *Hot Seat*, why won't the audience ever see her episode?

Supplementary Activities

1. Research: Have students watch the credits to their favorite television shows. They should make a list of each role that is necessary for the making of the program. Then, have them research the job descriptions for each role. Encourage students to present their findings in a creative format.

2. Drama: As a class, reenact the scene in which Stargirl pretends the Hot Seat is really on fire.

Chapters 13–15, pp. 62–75

Stargirl appears on *Hot Seat*, where the jury treats her rudely. The Electron basketball team enters the playoffs and begins to lose while Stargirl continues to cheer for both teams. She confesses her love for Leo by sending him a card, and he begins to fall for her.

Vocabulary
jabbed (65)
impish (66)
toggle (67)
cascade (68)
raucous (69)
prone (70)
volleys (71)

Discussion Questions

1. Discuss Stargirl's opinion regarding her name. Do you agree with Stargirl or the jury? *(Answers will vary. pp. 62–63)*

2. Discuss the irony surrounding Stargirl's answers to the jury's questions as compared to the way they treat her. *(Answers will vary, but should reference Stargirl's desire to make friends, which seems unattainable in the face of her peers' hostile attitudes. Discussions may also include the way Stargirl attempts to make friends, and why those attempts seem to have failed, succeeded, then failed. pp. 64–67)*

3. Stargirl's cheerleading attitude seems to change during playoffs. Discuss this change and why the crowd reacts to her as they do *(Stargirl no longer cheers for the other team as the playoffs progress. When the Electrons lose against Glendale, she cheers energetically, but unemotionally, only for her team. Frustrated at the loss, someone in the stands throws a tomato in Stargirl's face. She becomes the scapegoat for the team even though she has altered her behavior to satisfy her peers' demands. Discussions regarding "scapegoats" and people's inability to fully accept Stargirl will vary. pp. 68–72)*

4. Why is Leo afraid to tell Kevin about the card he received from Stargirl? *(Answers will vary, but may include that he is embarrassed that Stargirl likes him because she is currently unpopular. p. 73)*

5. Why does Leo react to the card from Stargirl as he does? *(Answers will vary, but should refer to the fact that he likes Stargirl in return. pp. 73–74)*

6. Discuss Archie's short lesson to the Loyal Order of the Stone Bone. *(Discussions will vary. Archie's words refer not only to the basketball team, but also to Stargirl. It is here that the author foreshadows that Stargirl will disappear in some way. p. 75)*

7. **Prediction:** Will a romantic relationship emerge between Leo and Stargirl?

Supplementary Activities

1. Research: Have students research the meaning of their names—first, middle, and/or last. They should write an essay outlining their findings and evaluate whether or not the meaning of their names accurately reflects their own personalities. If students think that their names are not accurate portrayals of themselves, they should suggest names that better represent their personality.

2. History: Have students research a person or group of people in history who held a belief or behaved contrary to popular opinion. Each student should give a presentation explaining the effects of this person's behavior/beliefs and any consequences that person might have faced as a result of their behavior/beliefs. (Examples: Rosa Parks, Galileo, etc.)

Chapters 16–18, pp. 76–99

Leo becomes infatuated with Stargirl, and they have their first conversation while Leo is crouched behind a car in her driveway playing with her rat, Cinnamon. Once they become a couple and begin spending time together at school, Leo realizes the other students are shunning them. He has joined Stargirl's isolated world, and Stargirl has found her friend.

Vocabulary
revving (77)
riddance (77)
acquainted (80)
crevices (82)
enchanted (85)
smitten (86)
dilapidated (90)
pleading (98)

Discussion Questions

1. Discuss how Leo describes Stargirl and her smile at the beginning of Chapter 16. How do you think he feels about Stargirl? *(says the smile puts sunflowers to shame, that it hit him hard, etc.; means he seems to like her, pp. 76–77)*

2. Discuss whether or not you think it is fair that Stargirl is kicked off of the cheerleading squad. *(Answers will vary.)*

3. When Leo visits Stargirl's house, he hides behind a car when she comes out. Why doesn't Leo stand up during his entire conversation with Stargirl? What would you have done in his situation? *(Answers will vary. pp. 79–83)*

4. Stargirl takes Leo to an enchanted place to do something he has never done. Though he is skeptical, Leo tries to "erase" himself. Discuss why you think Leo allowed Stargirl to introduce him to this new concept. Then discuss if you have ever done anything out of the ordinary because of someone else's influence on you. *(Answers will vary. pp. 90–94)*

5. Discuss how Stargirl's classmates are ignoring her. According to Kevin, what are their reasons? Do you agree or disagree with their behavior? *(Kevin says that she is shunned because of her cheerleading behavior. Her good deeds don't seem to outweigh the fact that she cheered for the other team when Mica was losing. Answers will vary. pp. 97–99)*

6. **Prediction:** Will Leo and Stargirl remain a couple now that they are both ignored by the student body?

Supplementary Activities

1. Drama: Allow two students to reenact the scene on pages 80–83 of the novel in which Stargirl and Leo have their first real conversation. As a class, discuss the awkwardness of the situation and why the author chooses to make this the first conversation between the two main characters.

2. Art: Have students review some of the poetic language the author uses to communicate how Leo feels about Stargirl. Then have students write a poem or make a collage that expresses what it feels like to be loved.

3. Literary Devices: Students should continue to analyze and interpret the analogies they locate in the text. **Similes**—"tension rising like fizz in a soda bottle" (p. 78); "her multicolored skirt looked like a pinwheel taffy" (p. 88) **Personification**—"the earth will touch us;" "universe will speak;" "stars will whisper" (p. 91) **Metaphors**—"the beacon of her smile" (p. 95); "the sea of tables and eaters" (p. 97)

Chapters 19–21, pp. 100–118

Leo discusses his conflicting emotions about Stargirl with Archie. Stargirl continues to advance in her oratorical competition. She also teaches Leo how to "see" and shares with him some of her secret ways of figuring out what people might need as Leo becomes Stargirl's pupil while observing people at a local mall.

Note: Following is a translation for the Spanish text found on page 104 of the novel: "It seems Mr. Borlock is the victim of a 'shunning' by his classmates at the high school. The main reason for the 'shunning' is Mr. Borlock's love interest, our very own Ms. Stargirl. He is in search of questions."

Vocabulary
excommunicated (100)
ambled (101)
mahogany (102)
derelict (104)
revel (107)
snit (108)
blotter (112)
facetiously (113)

Discussion Questions

1. Why isn't Leo satisfied with Archie's advice about Stargirl? *(Archie advises Leo to ignore Stargirl if he's only concerned with being popular, but Leo wants to be with Stargirl and still have friends. pp. 100–102)*

2. Why does Archie ask Señor Saguaro for questions rather than answers? What does this say about one of your own problems in life? Should you be asking for questions or answers? *(Answers will vary. p. 104)*

3. After consulting Señor Saguaro, Archie tells Leo that there is really only one question at stake: "Whose affection do you value more, hers or the others'?" Do you agree or disagree that this is the major question at hand? If you were in Leo's place, how would you answer this question? *(Answers will vary. p. 104)*

4. Discuss the types of conflict characters often face in literature—person vs. self; person vs. society; person vs. nature; person vs. person, etc. Then discuss the type(s) of conflict Leo is currently facing. *(Answers will vary. Students should discuss Leo's internal conflict and how external pressures, such as popularity and friendships with others, are affecting the conflict.)*

5. Describe some of the ways that Stargirl affects Leo and the way he views life. *(He laughs out loud for the first time, he begins to see the world in different ways, etc. Discussions will vary. pp. 106–111)*

6. If getting credit isn't Stargirl's motivation for doing kind things for others, what is her motivation? Would you do kind things for others if you knew you would never be recognized or thanked in any way? *(Answers will vary. p. 111)*

7. Contrast the ways that Leo and Stargirl view the world around them. Whose perspective on life would you rather have? (*While Stargirl sees the little things around her—notices on bulletin boards, people who rent romantic movies alone, ants, etc.—and does things for people without being thanked, Leo sees the things that are meant to be noticed—like the newspaper articles rather than fillers—and has a hard time comprehending why Stargirl wouldn't sign her name to a card or gift she left for someone. Answers will vary. pp. 106–118; throughout book*)

Supplementary Activities

1. Creative Thinking/Journalism: Stargirl shares with Leo how she would make decisions if she were editor of the *Mica Times*. Have students pretend that they are the editor of a local newspaper. Ask them what kinds of decisions they would make and what types of stories would appear on the front page. Then, have students submit a page of potential headlines for their newspaper.

2. Art: Have students draw caricatures of the woman (Clarissa) Stargirl and Leo follow while at the mall.

3. Literary Devices: **Similes**—"words...burrow like tiny eggs awaiting the rain of my maturity" (p. 103); "voice...as natural as a raven's caw or a coyote's howl at midnight" (p. 106); "as proud as a first-grader with a star on his paper" (p. 108); "search...like a prospector digging for gold" (p. 113) **Metaphors**—"the speech was...one creature's voice in the wild" (p. 106); "She was bendable light" (p. 107); "She was the Johnny Appleseed of loose change" (p. 117)

Chapters 22–25, pp. 119–138

Leo visits Stargirl's house, and they kiss for the first time. Stargirl makes a banner proclaiming her love for Leo and posts it on the school's major bulletin board for all to see. The shunning intensifies for Leo, and he begins to treat Stargirl differently. They have a long conversation regarding his desire for her to be more like "everyone."

Vocabulary
coasting (122)
cooed (125)
morale (127)
extravagance (130)
stoking (130)
torrent (131)
gumption (133)
hermit (136)

Discussion Questions

1. Leo is intrigued to see a bowl of hair and a wagon filled with pebbles in Stargirl's room. What do these objects say about Stargirl's personality? What items do you have in your own bedroom that say something about your personality? (*Answers will vary, but should suggest that Stargirl has emotions for herself as well as others. pp. 120–121*)

2. Though Leo continues to fall for Stargirl, he also continues to be bothered by the shunning at school: "I had never realized how much I needed the attention of others to confirm my own presence" (p. 126). Do you think that this statement is true for you? for most people? for a few people? Explain your opinion. (*Answers will vary.*)

3. On pages 127–128 of the novel, Leo summarizes some of the statements the students make about Stargirl. Do you agree or disagree with the students' opinions? Why do you think they hold these opinions? (*Answers will vary, but can refer to students who may feel guilty for being unkind. Rather than seeing her as selfless and themselves as selfish, they prefer to make her into someone who desires credit, the spotlight, glory, etc.*)

4. When Leo sees the sign Stargirl made him, he has mixed emotions. Even though he was initially thrilled to see the sign, why does he treat Stargirl rudely when she speaks to him later in the day? Discuss a time when you felt that your emotions were torn in opposite directions. *(Answers will vary. pp. 129–131)*

5. What is revealed about Kevin's character when he continues to eat lunch with Leo? *(Answers will vary. pp. 131–132)*

6. Leo laments when thinking about how people don't like Stargirl because she is different. Discuss Leo's point of view about belonging to groups. Do you agree or disagree with his point of view? Do you believe him when he says that he wouldn't change anything about Stargirl? *(Answers will vary. pp. 133–138)*

7. **Predictions:** Where did Stargirl go? Will she return?

Supplementary Activities

1. Creative Thinking: Ask students the following question: If you could devise a way to measure your own happiness, what would it be? Have them present their "happiness measures" to the class.

2. Writing: Write a journal entry from Stargirl's point of view the evening after she has the long talk with Leo about "everyone" and groups.

3. Literary Devices: **Similes**—"'Hi' was as rare as rain" (p. 131); "voice peepy like a little girl's" (p. 136) **Metaphor**—"linked myself to an unpopular person": crime (p. 132)

Chapters 26–28, pp. 139–156

Stargirl becomes "Susan" Caraway, a student who seems to behave like everyone else. Leo is her main teacher. Though she becomes "ordinary," she is still shunned by her classmates. However, Susan believes she will win their affection if she wins first place at the state oratorical contest. Leo accompanies her to the competition where he watches her outstanding performance.

Vocabulary
gawked (139)
strutted (140)
prominently (141)
rapped (146)
gander (147)
mesa (151)
rousing (154)
titters (155)
preamble (155)
primly (155)

Discussion Questions

1. Discuss why Leo is ashamed to be with Stargirl in front of his peers but is proud to be with "Susan" in front of them. *(Discussions will vary. pp. 139–140)*

2. Summarize Stargirl's transformation and Leo's role in it. What motivated the change? Do you think the change is better? Why or why not? *(Her talk with Leo obviously inspired change. She changes her appearance, her behavior, her diet, her preferences, her hobbies, and her name. Rather than dropping coins in a shopping mall, she shops for designer clothes. She wears makeup and follows Leo's lead on what "everyone" would do in different situations. Answers will vary. pp. 139–142)*

3. Why are the students still rude to Susan even though she is "one of them"? *(Answers will vary. pp. 142–143)*

4. What is making Susan sad enough to remove all but two pebbles from her happy wagon? *(Answers will vary. p. 143)*

5. Susan draws on her experiences to formulate her speech for the competition. Discuss the sources you use to prepare a paper or speech. *(Answers will vary.)*

6. **Predictions:** Will Susan win the oratorical competition? Will Mica give her a "hero's welcome" upon her return home?

Supplementary Activities

1. Public Speaking: Have students prepare speeches on topics for which they have a personal connection. Allot class time for each student to present his or her five-minute speech to the class.

2. Science: Have students research the moa or other extinct bird. They should make a collage that represents the bird's characteristics. Display the collages in the classroom.

3. Literary Devices: **Similes**—"spoke to me as if instructing a first-grader" (p. 147); "looked at [their roses] as if they were hand grenades" (p. 155)

Chapters 29–31, pp. 157–175

Susan wins the oratorical competition and returns home to a crowd of three. Disappointed by her welcome home, she decides to become "Stargirl" again, and she accepts the fact that Leo will not want to date her any longer. Leo does not attend the Ocotillo Ball, but Stargirl does, arriving alone but eventually attracting a train of Bunny Hop dancers who follow her outside for hours. Hillari slaps Stargirl when she finally returns to the school; Stargirl kisses her on the cheek and leaves the dance, never to be seen by any of the Mica Area High students again.

Vocabulary
dwindled (157)
asphalt (159)
gravitated (164)
disparaged (165)
castanets (165)
ember (167)
fronds (168)
disembark (168)
promenade (168)

Discussion Questions

1. Compare and contrast Susan's reaction to the crowd when she returns home to what you think her reaction would have been as Stargirl. *(As Susan, she is crushed that only a few people attend her homecoming. Regarding Stargirl's response, answers will vary. Suggestion: Stargirl would not have cared nearly as much about winning the award or being celebrated and would have been content that her best friends were there to cheer her on. Both "Susan" and "Stargirl" would probably have been happy to win. pp. 157–161)*

2. Why do you think Stargirl's father hands her silver plate to Leo? Why did it matter so much to "Susan" before arriving at the school but not to "Stargirl"? *(Answers will vary. Suggestion: For "Susan," her win was her ticket to popularity. The silver plate symbolized acceptance. When a crowd did not arrive to greet her, "Stargirl" realized her award could not ensure her popularity, and it lost its meaning. p. 161)*

3. Discuss Susan's quick transition to Stargirl. Do you think she truly became anyone else? *(Discussions will vary, but should note how easy it is for her to resume her former personality. Answers will vary regarding whether or not she ever truly abandoned "Stargirl." pp. 161–162)*

4. When Stargirl and Dori perform in the courtyard after school, why doesn't Leo cheer them on even though he feels it is the right thing to do? *(Answers will vary, but should reference his fear of rejection and the pressure he feels to dislike Stargirl. pp. 165–166)*

5. Stargirl makes an unusual entrance to the Ocotillo Ball. What do her appearance at the ball and the way she behaves say about her character? *(Answers will vary, but should mention her disregard for other people's opinions about her. pp. 167–175)*

6. What do you think compels so many students to follow Stargirl's lead during the Bunny Hop? Why doesn't Hillari join in? *(Answers will vary. Suggestion: Stargirl, though different, inspires people to more authentically express themselves. She appeals to their desires to break from the ruts of tradition and social expectations. Hillari is intimidated by Stargirl's ability to influence so many, and she sees no value in Stargirl's unique character. pp. 171–173)*

7. Why does Stargirl kiss Hillari on the cheek rather than slap her? Compare and contrast the values Stargirl and Hillari each hold. *(Answers will vary. Suggestion: Where Stargirl values love, peace, selflessness, and joy, Hillari values others' opinions of herself. Because Hillari's self-worth is based on what other people think of her, as well as her influence on other people, she is easily threatened by Stargirl's self-confidence and selflessness. p. 175)*

8. Why do you think Stargirl chooses the ball for her final appearance at Mica Area High? *(Answers will vary. p. 175)*

Supplementary Activities

1. Poetry: Have students write a poem about choosing between doing what is right and what people want you to do.

2. Arts: Invite students to research a specific type of dance and present their findings to the class. If possible, reserve an area where students can teach each other different dances. Allow them to play music so that they can demonstrate what kind(s) of music (appropriate for the classroom) is best for performing each dance.

3. Literary Devices: **Similes**—"plate...twinkled like a starburst in a galaxy of flashing cameras" (p. 157); "plate...rang like a dying bell" (p. 161); "moon rose into the sky like a lost balloon" (p. 167); "girl in chiffon...looked like a huge mint-green moth" (p. 172) **Metaphors**—dancing legs: flowery creature, fabulous millipede (p. 172); music: a tether, a kite string (p. 173)

Chapters 32–More Than Stars, pp. 176–186

Leo continues to visit Archie, and they continue to dwell on Stargirl's unique approach to life. Archie reveals to Leo that her office was in his toolshed, and when Archie is older, Leo accompanies him to bury a fossil (Barney). In his final reflections, Leo summarizes some of the ways Mica Area High has changed over time, and how Stargirl's legacy survives.

Vocabulary
primordial (177)
wistful (178)
municipal (179)
lark (184)

Discussion Questions

1. Discuss Archie and his sadness when trying to explain to Leo how much Stargirl cared for him. Why does Archie think Leo does not fully understand what happened? *(Answers will vary. Suggestion: Stargirl, who never changed, changed herself for Leo. Leo doesn't understand what kind of sacrifice Stargirl made for him because he isn't old enough to understand how important it is to be truly oneself. p. 178)*

2. What are your thoughts about Stargirl's office? How would you feel if someone you did not know had a personal file on you for the purpose of doing kind things for you? *(Answers will vary. For some students, knowing someone has a file on them makes no difference. Others may feel Stargirl invaded people's personal lives and might feel uncomfortable knowing someone had a file on them. pp. 178–180)*

3. On page 181 of the novel, Archie uses many phrases to describe Stargirl. Discuss what you think he means by each one. *(Answers will vary.)*

4. Why does Archie bury Barney? What does Barney's return to the ground symbolize? *(Answers will vary. Suggestion: Archie realizes that he is getting older and will soon pass on. As with Barney, he will return to the ground. New things will take his place, just as a new person moves into his house when he is gone, and an elementary school is built on Stargirl's enchanted place. pp. 182–183)*

5. Discuss the legacy Stargirl left at Mica Area High School and on Leo. What is a legacy? What kind of legacy would you most want to leave behind after you graduate? *(Answers will vary, but should reference how far Stargirl's legacy reaches. pp. 184–186)*

Supplementary Activities

1. Art: Have students write a poem or create a collage that explains who "star people" are. The finished product can define "star people" as a group or reflect on a single individual whom the student believes may fit the description.

2. Archaeology: Have students investigate the occupation of archaeology, including how to become an archaeologist, exactly what archaeologists do, and how the work of archaeologists has affected our world. Students may present their findings in a speech to the class, in essay form, or visually (film, poster, etc.).

3. Literary Devices: **Personification**—"smoke...paused as if to be admired" (p. 176) **Metaphors**—sun: melting butter (p. 177); echo of her laughter: second sunrise (p. 186)

Post-reading Discussion Questions

1. Discuss whether or not it was effective for the author to have Leo tell the story as an adult remembering the past. How did this choice add or detract from the book?

2. Discuss where you think Stargirl is 15 years after she leaves Mica Area High. What do you think she is doing? What do you think she calls herself?

3. How is Archie a significant character in the book? How would the book have been different without him? Would it have been better or worse? Explain.

4. Kevin never completely ignores Leo the way the other students do. Discuss why and what it says about Kevin's character and the friendship between Kevin and Leo.

5. Discuss what it takes to leave a legacy behind. How was Stargirl able to leave a legacy? Do you think she wanted to leave one? intended to leave one?

6. Reflect on what the phrase "fear of rejection" means. Compare your thoughts about this phrase before reading the book to your thoughts about it after reading the book. Have your thoughts changed? If so, how? If not, what reinforced them?

7. Discuss the pros and cons of being different. How would Stargirl be received in your school? Would you be proud or ashamed of this type of reception?

8. Throughout the book, the student body judges Stargirl, but she never judges others. Was the student body fair to Stargirl? Was Stargirl fair to them? Discuss the difference in these two behaviors and then evaluate whether or not there is ever an appropriate time to pass judgment on someone else's behavior.

9. What was the central conflict in *Stargirl*? At what point did the book reach its climax? How did the author bring resolution to the conflict?

10. Stargirl was least happy when she was trying to fit in and be "normal" like everyone else. Discuss why she was the most unhappy during this time, while Leo was the most happy. What does this say about their characters? Discuss what it means to "fit in."

11. Discuss popularity and whether or not it is valuable to pursue being popular. Be sure to list the pros and cons of being popular.

12. Discuss whether or not you would recommend this book to a friend. Why or why not?

13. Jerry Spinelli says that the ideas for this book began in 1966. Research popular opinions and attitudes from the 1960s. What elements of the 1960s are reflected in Stargirl's character? elsewhere in the book?

Post-reading Extension Activities

1. Write an essay explaining whether or not this book affected the way you see yourself. If it did, describe how your perception has changed, citing specific examples from the book that made an impact on you.

2. Write a poem or letter from Leo to Stargirl, written 15 years after he last saw her.

3. Draw a caricature of Leo, Hillari Kimble, or Archie. Write a short paragraph explaining why you accentuate the features you do.

4. Research to find a picture of a Paleocene rodent's skull. Create a sculpture of the skull. Name your sculpture.

5. Call several pet stores in your area. Create a chart listing how many pet rats each store sells, on average, in any given month. Based on your findings, develop a ratio that you think reasonably tells how many people, out of 100, own a pet rat.

6. Design a card for someone using nothing but geometric shapes. Inside the card, write a kind note, but do not sign your name. Secretly deliver the card to its recipient.

7. Organize a club similar to the "Sunflowers" for your school where each member must do something kind for another person each day.

8. Start a journal in which each entry reflects on decisions you made during the day. Evaluate why you made the choices you did and whether or not you are proud of your behavior. At the end of each week, write or revise basic guidelines that you hope to follow when making decisions.

9. Write about a day in Stargirl's life from Cinnamon's perspective.

10. Read the interview with Jerry Spinelli at the end of the book. Write him a letter expressing your opinion of *Stargirl* and ask three additional questions about the book or his profession that he does not address in the interview.

Assessment for *Stargirl*

Assessment is an ongoing process. The following ten items can be completed during the novel study. Once finished, the student and teacher will check the work. Points may be added to indicate the level of understanding.

Name _____ Date _____

Student   **Teacher**

_____   _____   1. Write a review of the book that includes general information about *Stargirl*'s characters, major themes, major conflicts, and setting.

_____   _____   2. Complete the Cause and Effect Map for *Stargirl* (see page 10 of this guide).

_____   _____   3. Correct any quizzes or exams taken over the book.

_____   _____   4. Complete two of the Post-reading Extension Activities (see page 24 of this guide). Present one of the assignments to the class.

_____   _____   5. Create a collage or painting of images and pictures that reflect Stargirl's character. Give your piece of art a title.

_____   _____   6. Complete the Characterization chart for Leo (see page 7 of this guide). Complete the chart a second time, identifying his character as an adult. Point out places where you think Leo is different as an adult than as a high school student based on the way his character narrated the book.

_____   _____   7. Write an essay identifying two major conflicts in *Stargirl*. Explain how each conflict is resolved.

_____   _____   8. Write an essay about the role of peer pressure in *Stargirl*. Explain how the forces of peer pressure influenced characters' decisions and how you think Stargirl was able, for much of the book, to remain disinterested in other people's opinions of her.

_____   _____   9. The book's final chapter is from Leo's adult perspective. Write an additional chapter of the book, from Stargirl's adult perspective of her high school experience.

_____   _____   10. Write a song or poem that emphasizes a major theme from *Stargirl*.

Glossary

Porcupine Necktie–Chapter 2, pp. 1–12
1. flourish (1): something done in a showy or ornate way
2. quills (2): stiff spines on a porcupine or hedgehog
3. milling (3): moving in a random or circular motion
4. keener (3): more intense; strongly felt or perceived
5. marooned (4): abandoned; isolated
6. plaited (8): braided
7. serenaded (10): sang to

Chapters 3–5, pp. 13–26
1. saguaros (14): thick cacti with spiny stems and white flowers
2. balking (14): recoiling; being taken away
3. amok (14): out of control or wild
4. perpetual (15): continual
5. flitting (15): quickly passing
6. aviary (16): a cage or building for housing birds
7. ambition (20): desire; goal
8. disdainful (21): aloof
9. converging (23): approaching; gathering around
10. antic (26): playful or ludicrous act

Chapters 6–9, pp. 27–42
1. ferociously (28): savagely; violently
2. blithely (28): carefreely; cheerfully
3. creodont (30): small, extinct carnivore with a small brain
4. proximity (30): nearness to
5. bafflement (32): a state of confusion
6. confirmation (32): verification; approval
7. charade (39): act; pantomime
8. acclamation (39): praise; strong approval
9. dormant (40): inactive; asleep
10. amorphous (41): without definition; shapeless

Chapters 10–12, pp. 43–61
1. yielded (43): gave in
2. lure (43): appeal or attraction
3. banishing (46): sending away alone
4. foreground (46): front
5. squabble (47): argument
6. mortified (48): very embarrassed
7. oblivious (50): unaware; not observant
8. hapless (51): unlucky; unfortunate
9. veterans (52): people with a lot of experience
10. mock (55): pretend
11. cued (56): signaled
12. maestro (58): a master of an art; a conductor of music
13. pantomime (61): act or gesture performed without words

Chapters 13–15, pp. 62–75

1. jabbed (65): poked
2. impish (66): mischievous
3. toggle (67): switch used to open or close an electrical circuit
4. cascade (68): fall
5. raucous (69): rowdy
6. prone (70): lying or facing downward
7. volleys (71): burst of voices all at the same time

Chapters 16–18, pp. 76–99

1. revving (77): running a motor loudly, usually while not moving
2. riddance (77): a removal of something unwanted or undesirable
3. acquainted (80): familiar with
4. crevices (82): folds; narrow openings
5. enchanted (85): charming; magical
6. smitten (86): sharply affected with great feeling
7. dilapidated (90): run down
8. pleading (98): begging

Chapters 19–21, pp. 100–118

1. excommunicated (100): cast out from a religious community
2. ambled (101): slowly walked; sauntered
3. mahogany (102): hard wood that is usually reddish-brown in color
4. derelict (104): abandoned; neglected
5. revel (107): to take much pleasure; to be merry
6. snit (108): fit; outburst
7. blotter (112): a book used to record events as they happen (e.g., arrests, fines, etc.)
8. facetiously (113): jokingly; humorously

Chapters 22–25, pp. 119–138

1. coasting (122): continue in motion, as down an incline, without much effort
2. cooed (125): said gently, softly, or lovingly
3. morale (127): mental condition relating to courage or confidence
4. extravagance (130): excessiveness
5. stoking (130): stirring up; feeding fuel to
6. torrent (131): violent flood or rush
7. gumption (133): willingness to take a risk; courage
8. hermit (136): a person who isolates him/herself from others

Chapters 26–28, pp. 139–156

1. gawked (139): stared stupidly
2. strutted (140): walked vainly; swaggered
3. prominently (141): noticeably
4. rapped (146): tapped; lightly, quickly, and sharply knocked
5. gander (147): a look
6. mesa (151): a high plateau with steep sides, usually covering a small area
7. rousing (154): stirring; lively
8. titters (155): nervous giggles

9. preamble (155): introduction
10. primly (155): formerly; properly

Chapters 29–31, pp. 157–175
1. dwindled (157): slowly decreased
2. asphalt (159): brown or black tar-like substance
3. gravitated (164): moved toward, as if pulled by an unseen force
4. disparaged (165): discredited; belittled
5. castanets (165): a musical device made of hard wood or ivory that attaches to the fingers and makes noise as it is clicked together
6. ember (167): piece smoldering among ashes or in darkness
7. fronds (168): leaves
8. disembark (168): unload or leave a form of transportation
9. promenade (168): walk taken for pleasure or to display finery

Chapters 32–More Than Stars, pp. 176–186
1. primordial (177): primitive; existing from the beginning
2. wistful (178): longing for
3. municipal (179): local; relating to a city or town
4. lark (184): a frolic; merry play